Machines On The Go

John Allan

First published in 2026 by Hungry Tomato Ltd
F15, Old Bakery Studios
Blewetts Wharf
Malpas Road, Truro
Cornwall, TR1 1QH, UK

A CIP catalog record for this book is available from the British Library

ISBN 9781835696736

Manufactured in the USA

Thanks to our editor, Julie Tofflemire

Discover more at
www.hungrytomato.com

Contents

Words in **bold** can be found in the glossary

The Mighty Mechanics

We are the Mighty Mechanics. Welcome to our workshop! We work on some amazing vehicles and machines. Here are a few of the tools we use to fix them.

A hex key is used to drive bolts and screws with hexagonal (six-sided) sockets in their heads.

We need these headphones to protect our hearing from loud noises.

We use a tape measure to make sure all the crops can fit in a truck.

This mallet can be used to break broken parts off a vehicle.

Rotary Rake

A rotary rake spins to gather hay into neat rows. It helps keep hay clean and dry.

The rows, called windrows, can be picked up by a baler (see page 8) later.

A big spinning wheel with arms moves close to the ground.

Baler

A baler gathers dried grass or hay and squeezes it into tight bundles called bales. Farmers use the bales to feed animals.

The baler rolls over rows of dry hay and scoops everything up.

The finished hay bale is pushed out of the machine!

In the chamber, the hay is packed tightly into a bale.

The feeder moves the hay inside the baler.

Bale Wrapper

A bale wrapper covers hay bales in plastic. This keeps the hay dry and fresh so that animals on the farm can have food even in winter.

The wrapped bale is ready to be stored for later.

In-line bale wrappers make long rows of wrapped bales.

A sharp **blade** cuts the plastic.

Rollers spin the bale while plastic from a big roll is wrapped around it.

Forklift

A forklift lifts and moves heavy farm supplies like hay bales, seed bags, and tools. It makes carrying things much easier!

The arms lift the items up or down on the mast.

Two flat, metal forks at the front slide under items.

This forklift is moving a stack of hundreds of onions!

A heavy block at the back keeps the vehicle from tipping forward.

Telescopic Handler

A telescopic handler – or telehandler – is like a forklift but with a long arm. It lifts things high up or far away.

This telescopic handler is moving bales of hay.

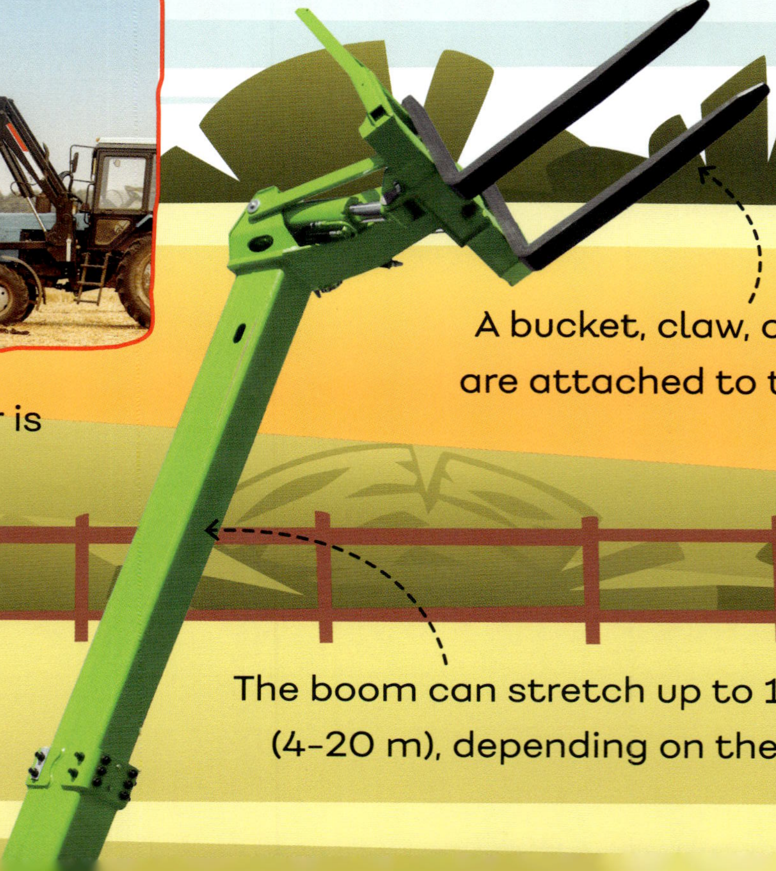

A bucket, claw, or forks are attached to the top.

The boom can stretch up to 13–65 feet (4–20 m), depending on the model.

Special legs called outriggers can extend out to the ground to make the vehicle more stable.

Grain Cart

A **grain cart** carries harvested grain from the field to a storage area. It can hold a lot of grain.

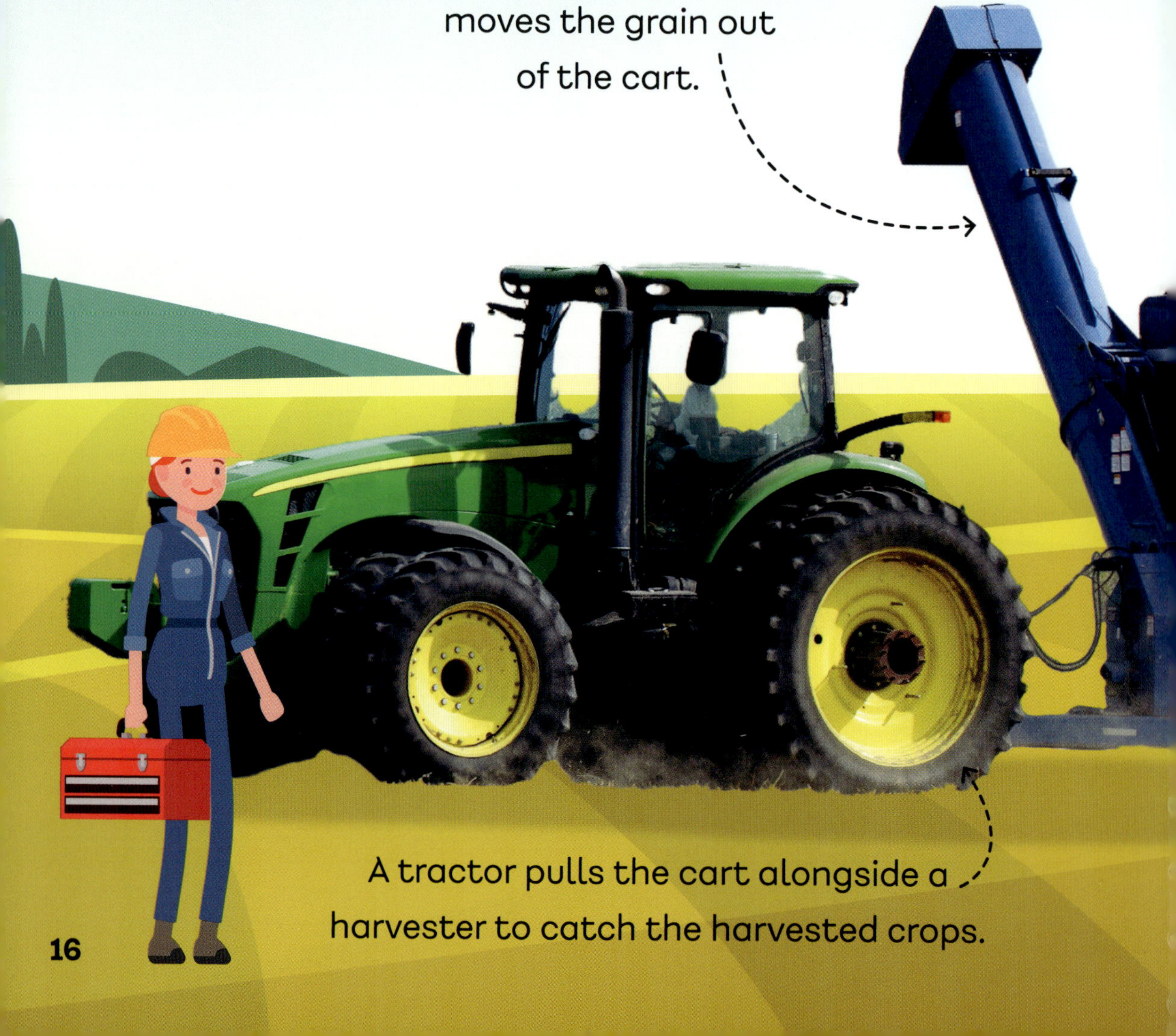

Once the grain is collected, an **auger** moves the grain out of the cart.

A tractor pulls the cart alongside a harvester to catch the harvested crops.

This grain cart is helping a combine harvester with the corn harvest.

Grain is caught and stored in the hopper, ready to be moved off the field.

Grain Auger

A grain auger is a long pipe that moves grain into **silos**, trucks, or bins. It gets the grain from the ground to a higher place.

This grain auger is filling a silo with grain.

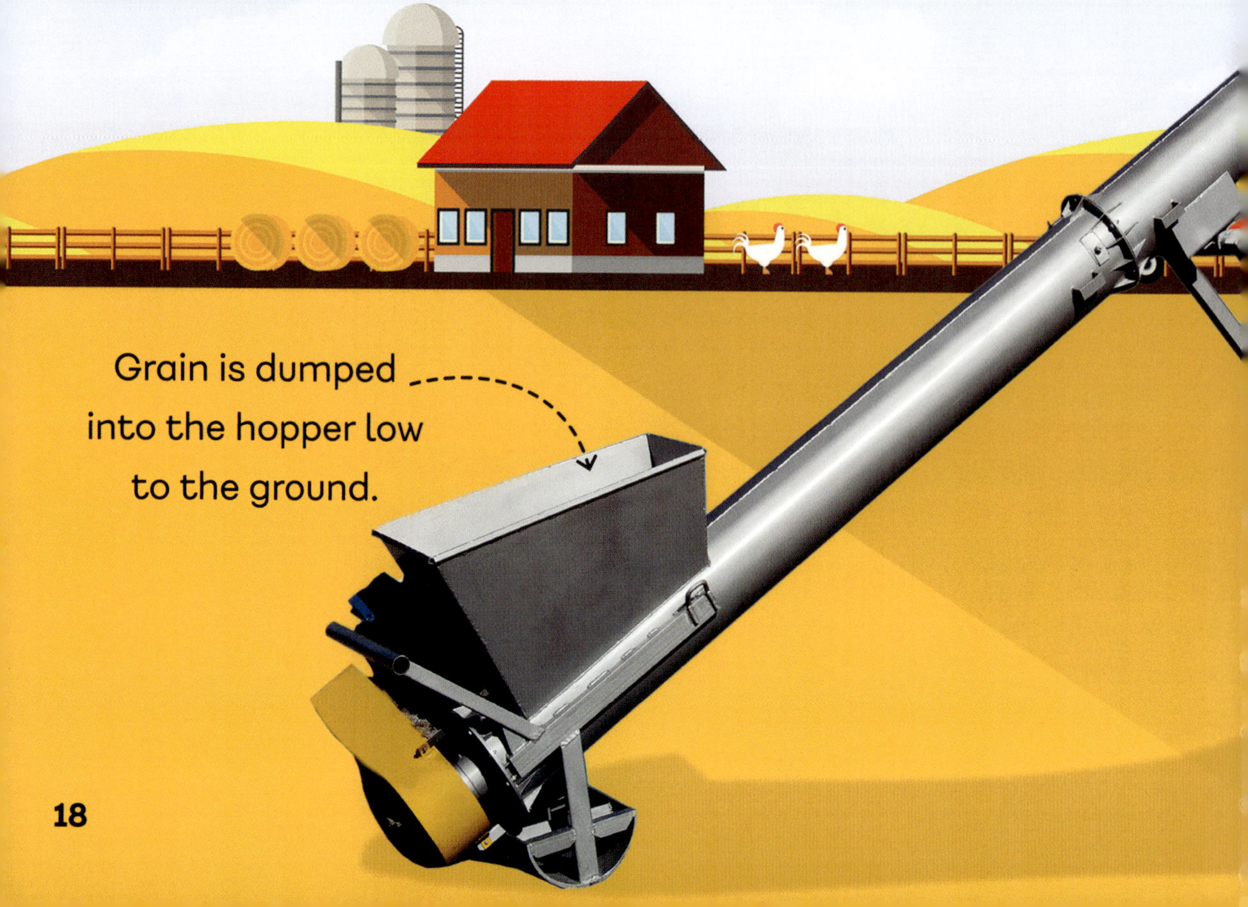

Grain is dumped into the hopper low to the ground.

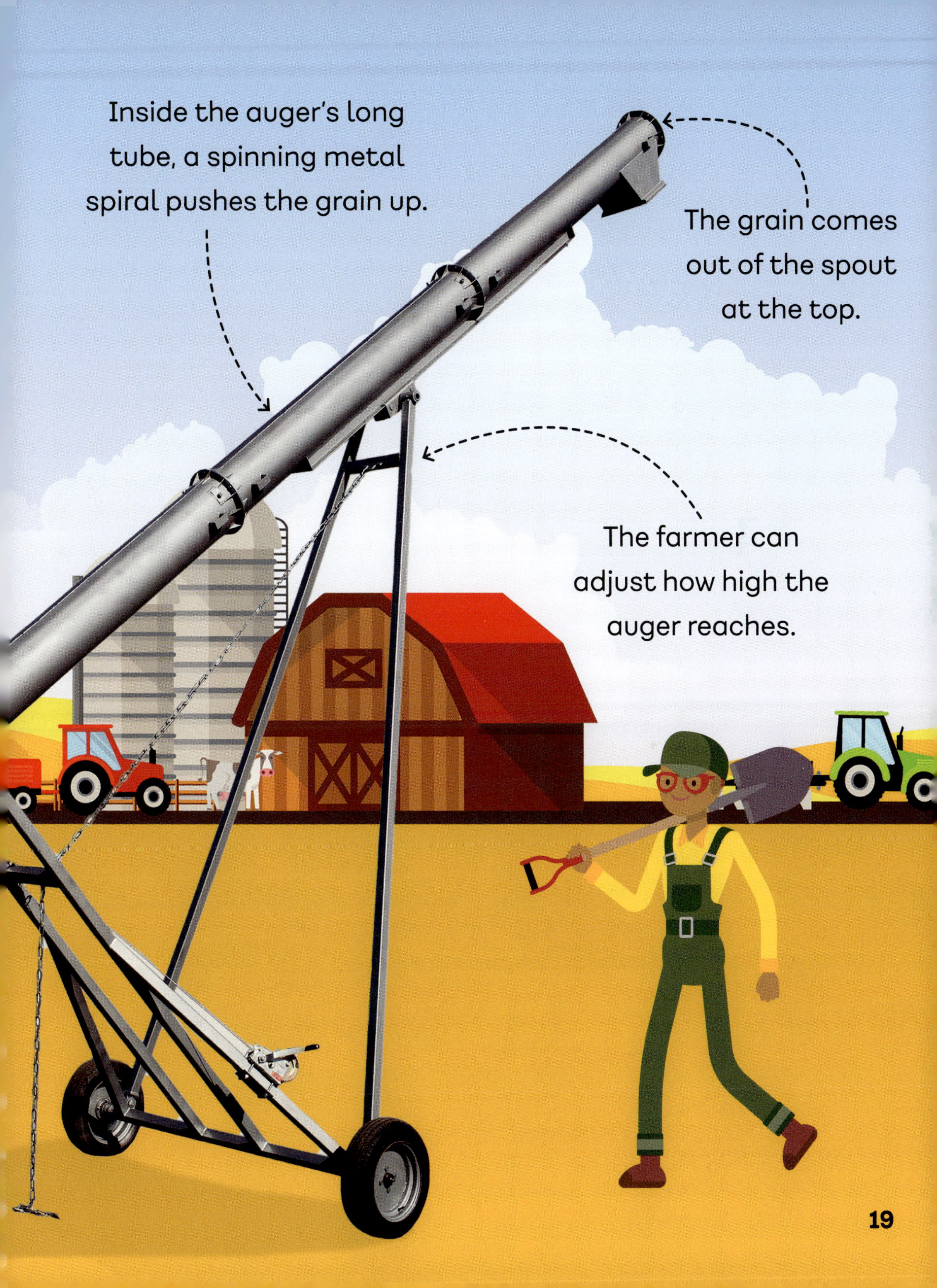
Inside the auger's long tube, a spinning metal spiral pushes the grain up.
The grain comes out of the spout at the top.
The farmer can adjust how high the auger reaches.

Milk Tanker

A milk tanker is a huge truck that carries fresh milk from farms to factories. It keeps the milk cold and safe along the way.

A special layer of **insulation** around the tank keeps the milk cold.

A pump pushes cold milk through hoses into the tank.

The milk is pumped back out again when it is delivered.

Drivers have to be careful because milk can **slosh** around while turning or braking!

The tank can hold 5,000 gallons (22,730 L) of milk or more!

Livestock Transporter

A livestock transporter is a special truck that moves cows, pigs, and other farm animals.

The animals ride in a big metal box called a trailer.

Fresh air flows through **ventilation** holes in the side of the trailer.

Ramps at the back help the animals to walk into or out of the trailer.

Walls inside the trailer keep the animals in smaller groups.

Glossary

Auger – a tool shaped like a screw that can dig holes or move things through a tube.

Blade – flat, sharp tools for cutting.

Grain – small, hard seeds from food plants such as rice or wheat.

Insulation – a material that is wrapped around something to stop heat, electricity, or sound escaping or entering it.

Silos – tall towers that are used for storing grain.

Slosh – when substances that flow freely, like milk, move carelessly or noisily.

Ventilation – the fact of letting fresh air come in and move around.

Picture Credits
(abbreviations: t = top; b = bottom; m = middle; l = left; r = right; bg = background)

Wikipedia: By Wikideas1 - Own work, CC0 11tr. Shutterstock: 21tl. Alfmaler 6-7bg, 14-15bg; Amanita Silvicora 12-13bg; Anastasiia Kozubenko 22-23bg; Andrew Rybalko (characters throughout); Another77 12-13m; B Brown 18tl; David BISE 7tl; Droidworker 10-11bg, 18-19bg; Dvande 16-17m, 17tr; Edge Creative 8-9bg; Gozzoli 6-7m; KonstantinChristian 14ml; KOTOIMAGES 20-21m; Miguel Perfectii 22-23m; Nidvoray 18-19m; Photobac 8m; ProStcokStudio 20-21bg; RGTimeline 13tr; Sheryl Watson 10-11m; Varga Jozsef Zoltan 8tl; Vector_Vision 16-17bg; Vereshchagin 9m.